THE SELECTIVE MEMORY OF THE SUBCONSCIOUS

FOREST GREENWELL

Dedicated to Pam and Roger for being my biggest supports, sources of inspiration, and for showing me what comedic relief is.

To my lover, who everyday reminds me that the best and the most human versions of myself are often the same; and the other lovers that had me feeling it all for many years.

LESSONS
LEARNED
(ORPENDING)

I

SILLY BOY
YOU BELIEVE THE MOON
CAN MOVE WATER?

BUT NOT
CHANGE YOUR HEART WHEN
JUPITER IS ASCENDING?

WHAT SHAME
TO BE SO LONELY IN
YOUR OWN UNIVERSE.

DOES LOVE
NOT CHANGE THE RHYTHM
OF YOUR HEART?

WHY BELIEVE
IN ANY KIND OF MAGIC
THAT IS "LOGICAL"?

HOW DESPERATE
TO TRUST THAT FATE
HAS A PLAN.

WHO TOLD
YOU THE STARS SHINED
JUST FOR US?

THE STARS
DO NOT KNOW YOU,
THEY MADE YOU.

Stop telling lies. Fold up your love, throw it in a bag.

I want you to leave. Take your knock off affection,
it's giving mine a bad reputation.

Knowing they will lose you, & not caring until they do

"next question". I hear myself say it often. evasive, in my silence. persuasive, in the three consonant sound; that glance that feels like a glare. i am as absent in talk as you are now. i spoke too much too soon. you need to catch up, your pace is fast but you're beating off track.

but it's fine. it's totally fine.   even though i never thought i would be the kind of girl that had a lover that never called. but i guess we're just friends, and those we do not call back. often. enough time in between to realize there is not a kind of person that doesn't get called, only a person who never calls. and i am both of them as you are both of them. i'll try to be around to answer.

neither of us should (or will) make any promises. my willingness to forge them forgets that you are not as bound to receive as i am to keep. and as you have made none yourself, it makes the ones i've made up more fragile to the beats they take without their upkeep.

we respectably accept that respect was respectively uninvolved. it was given without a cause, so this pause - this absence - this void of silence that probes at the walls of respectable behaviour, is proving harsher to harness into a narrative that does not sound delusional in my own mind that dwales on how to turn this into a story instead of another lesson to learn.

when i thought you could love me, so i loved you first

If you are the type of person who utters no when I ask to pick flowers from strangers gardens in the middle of a rainy night with the same lips that want to kiss me, be warned. I will make you hate yourself for ever wanting to love me, make you loathe every single time you said no because yes would have been easier than the disappointment in my eyes upon realization that you are not the type of person I want to fall in love with me. If you are the type of person that bends to my every whim and desire even to put your own aside, be warned. I will make you regret the day I was a still a stranger and you listened when I told you to kiss me, make you fear my boredom in you more than my sadness from neglect while you wish we had never met because the tears I'm crying are from your hands that hold my face but can't touch my mind between them.

Ah, there is no winning.

You'll hate me because you love me, but you'll love me just the same.
Forget about yourself; you're lost to me.

The Type of Person

Inside out. Smeared on walls, canvas, journals. A bloody piece of "art". Not red but black and blue. Inconsistent and non-blandiloquent. Falling apart how snow falls from the sky, hitting the ground like tears running from eyes. This is what happens when you ask someone else to fix you – they get bored and you look fun and here's the thing...

Here's the thing...

The things is, these people aren't engineers. They are gamblers and prostitutes and homeless and they will use you, not build you up. You will not be featured in a gallery, just a grave. And this is incipient. The only fixing to be had are the patches in their own lives: the plug in the hole in the dam(ned), and all the pressure is on you. You are not a corner, not a game, not a home. You are used, black, and blue.

These Are Not Artists

Twice I turned my back on you. Two times I was so blue I had to kiss the red from others lips just to understand that those two colours made the same purple of the bruises I was covered in. Twice I was a reminder that the thorns of rose petals hide in unlikely places, that they will bite your skin drawing poison to the surface making your words black. Two times I drowned you in sweet lies, had you convinced that if the surface reflected it was pure. You saw yourself and I know you're no saint so twice I was the alarm, going off a little too late.

Tulips for A Rose (About R, R & M)

jealousy is a hot water splash, love uncontained surging from my vena amoris in spiked waves to my finger tips tainting the things i touch (even you). because love uncontained is as rampant as rage & i don't know how to quell that either.

anything that you belonged to before i abhor because it means you do not belong completely to me. not that i want to own you - that's too much responsibility for someone that can't even carry all of herself. and you know, i want you to love with all of the lessons of other loves, just not with them towed along.

you are a tug ship; a freight train. with so many cars between us that the closest i feel to you is at a u-turn. and at the end i have the power - the capability to pull my own way. but truthfully there's enough of that view that i've seen before; seen the postcards so i can decide not to miss it that much. and you still have the momentum. i have strength but not to start an uphill battle after a dead stop. and anyway, maybe we will crash like a high-speed, metal wave into a mountain because it seems that there is nothing else in the world that can stop this.

sometimes it feels easier to love the wrong one, then to not love at all

Sometimes it's more that you're missing the part of yourself that was taken when they left, rather than the thief themselves. You jump every time your phone buzzes hoping it's a message from that piece reassuring you it is safe now in hands more gentle than the ones that took it from you, that it is being put to good use. That although there was no instruction manual, it found it's place quite nicely nuzzled in another chest. And that it misses you, but somehow feels it is better off. You look at the patchwork that is yourself and all of who you are that is bits of other people while trying to remember if that was ever a part of you that you had a right to let be taken away – that's what it was, wasn't it? Taken? Or was it ever even yours to own? You are emptier now, a little lighter. A little heavier in the parts around this now gaping hole. But hopefully the next lesson will fit nicely in that cave. Hopefully it is something the skin of your soul won't reject.

Not A Bullet Hole

in three weeks you will miss her -
so bad.
like your body after a sugar crash
and you will eat up any sweetness
that crawls your way.
hunting down Swedish berries and lovers that
still love you because they taste
like the first time
you reunited.

and you have no idea what to look forward to
next time - there has to be a next time.
because she's left you full of cavities
and her skin is the only softness
that knows how to fill those holes

lest all your good intention slowly
leak out
leaving the nerves exposed.

is there insulin for love?

When they don't call, remind yourself
you never expected them to
and the flaws you refused to see in them
are ones you will no longer have to ignore. Forgiveness is
sometimes a better fantasy
than longing, and
reality likes to make us diabetics
before we can eat the cake it gives us.

the five month long one-night stand

Sometimes the water running through my pipes sounds like crickets when it's early spring and you forget how to listen properly and you get hopeful that your wishing finally brought you somewhere far away, and you're too kind to tell yourself the reality. Especially after a boy that smells like sweat and sugar and who's kisses taste like vanilla just left, you realize this all must be a dream because boys only taste so good after ice cream or when they are thinking about you when they fuck someone else. And he is not here when you wake up and your teeth do not ache so it must mean that the spring you feel is blooming inside of another. So you are still here, but you crossed the line. You are still here, and you are still fine.

a lover told me to be in the presence of a moth
was to be in the presence of knowledge
my roommate scours the house
to kill them.
they live in dark places,
cocooning themselves and i wonder
if a bulb is enlightenment or a beacon to death.

is it ignorance with which they eat
my shirt, or do they know
it is outdated anyway?
do they burrow in my oatmeal
knowing i need more protein or
are they just ignorant of where they lay?

Conflicts About Moths

I am sorry, for today somebody asked me what
kind of a person I was
- a somebody in my head -
and I realized that I am no one type of person.

That this same body will say yes to you
and no to you,
that in any non-movement there is grace
as much as there is me losing balance.

You were never the type to be reduced
to what I did and didn't need,
and you are the kind of person you need to be.

Abrasive, gentle, a hard current or
 a calm breeze.
Adapting.
You are not the kind of person,
but a person of different kinds;
and I'm sorry that, until now,
I had not thought to realize.

I used to want to hurt on purpose because I thought that made sense of hurting without control. I would wallow in the simplicity that all life really is, is what is happening now. I would think about what follows. I would think about the love I have, and how one day it would turn to pain. I would think about the home I've built, and (like all the others) there would come I time I would have to leave again. I would think so far ahead that I could remember a loneliness I do not yet know, and envision all that I would probably miss but skipped the parts that made it so. I do things that I know will sting, like go through photographs. Pictures of the one I love, with another that used to make him laugh. I do not know what in me changed, or if maybe I just like my present now. But when I start to wade those waters, I can float instead of sinking to the bottom. You can delve as deep as you can hold your breath, but the bottom is dark and in grasping for answers all you come back with is a hand of sand. It slips through your fingers like the time wasted; the time it took to learn to swim. The only control there really is, is the acceptance of how things are. Not the resolve of giving up, but the strength to keep moving on. There may be fate, or fairness, or logic. There may be none at all. The only thing I know is there is enough pain in the world without bringing it on.

When we go looking for things we cannot find to make us feel like we got something right

MY FATHER LOOKS LIKE JESUS

SO I STOPPED BELIEVING

IN GOD.

Daddy Issues

THE SOFT
LOVE
(AND OTHER EASE)

2

I MUST LOVE YOU, I AM
TOO SMALL TO CONTAIN
ALL THAT I CAN PRODUCE.
IT MUST BE YOU, I AM TOO
SELFISH TO NOT CHOOSE
WHOM IT GOES TO.

I'm not surprised there isn't yet a word that embodies him. One must be venial to our language because it is missing a lot of them. Full of labyrinthine, mellifluous, effervescent words but none of them conflate to an equivalent of you. None feel quite right pounding themselves off my tongue, getting caught between my teeth, bubbling out of my mouth as I stumble over the assonance and cajole the vowels with what I'm praying is proper diction. They are amiable in my mind but hostile between my cheeks. I can't figure out if you're long or short, if you should rhyme or acquiesce to leave my lips. My mind dwales while I try to appease it, but I need to be candor.

Mel-au-thi-ous

adjective

- One who makes you feel like spring
- The physical embodiment of eunoia

I tasted myself

on your mouth.

It was the first

time I knew

warmth was a

flavour.

I want to be touched with good intention, trying too hard to make you not want me. Not putting forth effort into being easy to understand, saying things like "I want to be heartless" without explaining that I just want to give all of myself away.

I am altruistic in my absence, appealing to my need to appease people. It is easier to now make you angry than to later make you sad. It is better to have no hook at the end of a line than to have to rip it from you when it is time to let go - instead just giving you the freedom to fall when you want.

It is a graceless dance between grateful people, understanding that although we may not move well, at least we can move. Even so, words come out abrasive and thoughts may be ugly. But it is guarded by intention and I like it when you massage my head.

Intent

There's a trail tattooed on your skin where my fingers have ventured over your shoulder and across your collar bone.

I want to travel your body, write my own map. Follow your mineral trail of sun spots splattered on your back, guided by the North Star freckles on your right arm.

I want to know every story of every scar as deeply as if they were a river I could swim in, I want to conquer every peak of your body over and over again.

I want to feel at home on your mouth, know I'm welcome when my name tolls from your voice.

I want to be the light that spreads in the darkness of your heart in the cave that is your ribcage. I want to breathe in every stalagmite of smoke that leaves your lungs and tell love stories to the moon in your eyes.

The arches of your feet are valleys I want to sleep in and I want to press every wild flower I see in the crevices that your joints make into a dictionary of words that don't yet exist that are the explanation of how my tongue feels on your teeth. There's a trail tattooed on your skin that my fingers will never stop treading.

Bone Trail

I am sorry
to those I love
that I told I did not trust

It's not untrue
in a way, like all ways
but it is not the whole
story
either.

I cannot blame those
who came before you for
how I feel now
but

The lack of trust
is in myself
because

just once blinded by love
was blindsided enough.
But it wasn't just once,
or twice,
thrice -

I can't tell you how many
times I fell
head over heels.

The many times
I didn't know
how close I was
to the bottom.

Forgive me for looking
too far ahead,
getting too close
to the edge -

Because even if the end
is near, I would like to
know
if below

Will break my bones,
or drown me.

Maybe there will be
a bridge to cross,
a parachute on my back

But what if it breaks,
doesn't open,
there isn't time?

I'd rather have
the nerve
to jump

Than to lose my breath
in the onset
of a fall (or a push).

Cliff Jumping

You swear that if he stood in the West that's where the sun would rise. Then you remember that you're also watching a sunset from the wrong side of the world. Now you wonder if a ball of fire in the sky wants to resign it's position. You think that if you saw a new colour for the first time it would feel the same as when you saw him for the third, and the thirtieth, and the three-hundredth time. Then you remember that pink used to be your favourite, but now it's green. You realize it's not the pigments that have changed, but you. You think about how when the sun sleeps you love red, but when it wakes you love lavender; so somewhere in-between, your dreams must have turned blue. You wonder if you can commit to rise and set like the sun and moon do.

Rising Change

I am thankful my heart was beating fast enough to believe that moment was **the** moment. My hands were shaking the way they do when you're trying to use frozen fingers to send a message.

...

How much did you pay for me to watch a stage out of the corner of my eye? Your laugh was better than the commentary.

...

We could have eaten grilled cheese. The lighting wouldn't change the way I looked at you.

...

You keep saying "I like you so much" and I keep wondering if you're waiting to say what that really means.

...

The kisses haven't changed I just feel better knowing you want me.

...

You ask me what's wrong and I say "I think I love you" and you say "Well, tell me when you know."

Falling In Love
M.D.

I wonder if it's difficult for the sun to rise every morning, if he has a routine of coffee or a snooze button he allows himself to press only three times. I wonder if he knows how even though there is challenge in change, the sky is so beautiful. And I wonder if he's still lovers with the moon, or do we only have the night because they grew apart. Is it awkward for him to see her in the sky sometimes before he's settled for the night? Does he choose the colours he paints the sky with every night?

I wonder if he's sleeping angry when he set's bright red. I wonder if he misses her when he wakes up tangerine.

I worry for the moon, carrying around the weight of the tides. I wonder how she got tied down and if she's just strong or determined. I worry for all the blame we put on her for our grievances when she's full, if she's ever confessed to such mischief or simply never denied the accusations. I wonder if she is vying for the sun's affections with every wax and wane, trying to please his appetite.

I worry the stars are too far away to be friends. I worry she can't see her reflection in the ocean.

Caring For The Sky

We make love with loud laughter and morning voices. With arcane apologies and face-cupped sleeps. We make love with our eyes dancing to meet each other across a crowded room and playing piano keys with fingers while our hands are embraced. Every desire I have for you adds to it an increment, and I still need the stars because I need to do everything on earth with you and then some, but know that you're the only reason I need anything more than you. We are enough – all the poems of other people, and dreams, and realities in a concentrated cough syrup to soothe the aches I have for you. We don't have to touch but we make love and I will embezzle your attention to make a currency in aureate messages just to buy it back again. Whenever I am reminded of you, we make love and I'll find you everywhere - in everything - just to do it again.

Making Love - Mediocre Recipe
M.L.

This is not a love story.

This is not a poem, or a novel, or a song. I don't know what it is but it is none of those things.

What this may be, though, is a collection. A collection of explanation, and occasionally some apologies.

Like how I am sorry that when I am with you I often can't speak because the words in my mind don't come out as smoothly as they are thought, and how my tongue trips over them. They are prisoners running and running and slamming hard into my teeth; getting caught. And when I kiss you I'm trying to release them and I hope that these words run through your bloodstream and that you understand and when I bite your lip I'm trying to get the residue of the vowels out of my mouth before they become to sweet and let me rot.

When you question me for how I look at you and I tell you it's nothing, follow your gut. You know what I'm thinking. I'm sorry I lie. I can't handle the truth. You know what I'm thinking. I'm afraid it's too much, that it will come down like a tidal wave and we will not be strong enough breakers. I'm sorry I'm not afraid to feel but that I am afraid to speak. I'm sorry there is any fear in me at all, and if I can console any hurt let it be that I also feel safe. With you.

For every time I pick a fight, know I am picking you. For every time I am short on words, on breath, on life - understand that I sing to the fucking moon every night you are not with me hoping that one day I will make it up to you because I am not lacking in determination what I am lacking in courage.

And while the moon is encouraging others, I praise every cloud that crosses the sky because I don't want you to see me for what I am, and I am jealous of every ray of light that gets to touch you in places I cannot, when I cannot. And it's so sadistic that I love that you're broken but the thing is I don't think you'll cut me up. Despite your warning label you've been an emollient to yourself and your rough edges have been smoothed out. I want to drink you up like too much of a good thing; I think that would be the best way to go.

When I wake up in the morning I don't think about how lucky I am. I don't think about your face or that I want to touch your hip. I think about how soft your eyes feel on mine and how this is the one thing I never dreamed of and the one thing I never want to lose.

Am I doing this right yet? I'm sure it isn't a love story.

You Know What I'm Thinking, But This Isn't What You Think

Do you ever come into abrupt consciousness because of the mundane? You are walking. Walking. Legs moving automatically. Feel the weight of your thighs and the flexibility in your hips. Moving forward. A pace.

How can we remember to fidget and blink and lick our lips, but somehow it is so easy to forget how to breath? A thing I never notice until I feel a little sick to my stomach and realize I am taking in air at about 10% of my lungs maximum capacity.

And those little lies. The ones you don't have to tell, that don't spare anyone or change anything. The kind of 2$ on a large purchase that doesn't make a difference but you still feel better lowering it a little or raising the stakes an inch. When you say "I love you" automatically because you mean it, but in that moment out of nowhere you're not really feeling it. And you become aware of how many times you may have done that, said that. The way the things we once appreciated and were so new and sometimes hard are now second nature. Except breathing still.

Except the first thing we ever did other than scream. Right out of the womb before we knew we had eyes to open and a world to see, the air was the first step to feed the lies and I love you's and to pump blood through our legs.

Air either in waves of too much or too little. We complain it is dirty, stagnant, hurting our noses or we revel for a moment in the freshness of spring in the country and maybe give a single thought to running. Or screaming. Or holding it all in. And then it becomes easy to forget again. But we keep moving forwards and backwards without thinking or feeling at all, and it's funny how pain is what brings us alive but happiness is what keeps us sure that there is nothing really going on at all.

Selective Memory of The Subconscious

WHERE IS THE SCIENCE TO EXPLAIN FINDING GOD IN SOMEONE'S EYES JUST TO PRAY TO HIM THAT YOU NEVER HAVE TO SEE THEM FOR THE LAST TIME?

Inconclusive Research for An Atheist

NO LONGER LOVE & IT'S REPLACEMENTS

3

I WANT TO SPIT YOU OUT
LIKE A GOOD TASTE
GONE STALE.
EVERYTHING I THOUGHT
I WOULD ALWAYS LOVE
& NOW I CAN'T STAND

When I asked him if he was seeing other people I
mistook his distance from the population as affection
for me. Or maybe he lied.
I felt so close to him, I trusted his body more than my
mind. Actions speak louder than words but that doesn't
always mean they speak the truth.
I trusted he knew not to hurt me when he asked about
my father and he held my face and told me I was
beautiful. He was never sober.
His look of understanding wasn't for me, but for
himself - knowing he would just be another
of the stories I tell so they don't haunt me.

B.A.

There is a man in the corner, he says he's made of
memories.
And when someone pops their head into the kitchen
you're just doing dishes,
but this self-proclaimed memory man is taunting you
while he hangs from the ceiling out of sight.
Torturing a part of you,
maybe an alternate in another realm of time.
Maybe the part of you that's just beyond the mirror.
Late at night when you're dreaming he's the shadows in
your night mares,
the grey light that makes you unsure of the time before
sunrise in the morning,
the acid chewing at your stomach when you've forgotten
to eat again.
He says he's made of memories,
but only of a certain kind.
Be weary of the ways you are deceived.
He is made of regrets.

The Past Wears a Mask

We met online, typical of our time. We went pool hopping, I met you at 1AM on our bikes with a bucket for the slide. You came over and left at 3. How fitting that for 3 months I saw you every week. I left whatever "this" ever is after our best evening - after many years of practice I could finally hit a high note. Before you left we said good-bye at the same place we left it off because it's easier to relive memories than to keep making new ones. We fucked, after undressing on the roof in the rain. And you stayed for brunch a week before I fell in love with what a person was giving me, not what I couldn't have.

S.H.

I wonder when you tell me
I'm the best, how many comparisons
you had to make.
In your catalogue of used to be lovers,
how many times did you flip the page?
To discern that I'm on top?
And I'm curious about this statement,
the truth of it -
if you're lying to me or just yourself?
Or maybe I just don't trust the statement
all that much because
when I say it too, I mean it whole heartedly.
And statistically one of us has to be a liar.

D.A.

If my teeth were made of glass
I'd shred the words I say to hurt you

Turning "I don't love you"s into
"Told you no lie"s
And bite my tongue to taste the blood

I'll let the ridges cut you when I lick your wounds
Ink dripping from your ears
But my bitter sorry's would come out ugly
And salt makes me vomit

The fire in my mind doesn't burn your skin
And the smoke won't make you tear
You're black with soot while I dig your grave
for a diamond

And you don't know it as I bite your shoulder
There's a taste of my own medicine gone rancid
This is when I learned not to swallow
I'd rather hurt you than heal myself

Intentions Of Healing

There have been many times I've tried again, but when you lost your patience you also lost your rights. I "learned" my lesson but not the exceptions. I never knew I didn't want someone who would demand me, it was a new thing. I let you discover what a mouth could do and I let you know I hated your bed. And after I deleted you, was still thinking about you, always felt like there was a part of me needing you - I thought we could be friends.

But we still fight like love hurts
are intimate like lovers
make me feel like I come first
and I did come first
that one night I fell head first

I tell you my fear is I might love another but not that you might be the one that I covet, and it's good that you keep your distance because when I am near you the feeling is instant. But you don't belong here; in this city, in this country, in this heart. We are still friends , it tears me up less than being apart.

You will love someone in Paris one day
L.T.

You left the friendship door open and then fucked my
best friend through the frame. When I slammed it shut I
realized it was made of glass, anyway. And when I left the
province you still walked my dog, and when we switched
places you called my sister up and it's like how can you
want everything in my life but me? And I asked myself
that for too long before realizing you aren't the kind to
realize someone needs an apology.

And it's like, I didn't even want this? I just wanted to
fuck? But you broke into my apartment and left a cake in
my freezer and a note on my laptop.

So when years later I get a message saying you never did
anything wrong, I just want to let you know that co-
dependancy was not a path I wanted to walk.

I could say sorry for the dozen other things that hurt you,
but for years after your grandfather died you still
wouldn't take your grandmothers calls and I realized that
you hurting wasn't always me doing something wrong.

C.L.B.

your intentions as soft as your hands
impermanent and fleeting
ghosts of your touch lingers
but that's all
as fast as you came you're gone
and what's wrong (?)
       is that I always wanted to be haunted
but never by such... gentle means
though I can't dismiss these dreams
I can tell myself it means nothing.
I can't control the way you leave
and have left.
I can tell myself it means nothing.

And when he was happy it was like sitting next to the
sun.
You burned with the fire he was comprised of, and
shone on everyone making them beautiful.
He made people beautiful. And when he
left everyone was dull. Maybe they
were always dull. Maybe we
never saw them properly
because we were so
preoccupied, we
were burning.
But he was
the only one
who burned
away.

We Were Burning
B.N.

if you had a grave id dig it up and kill this at the root. I can't let these thoughts grow anymore, like ivy crawling up the walls of my skull, patiently waiting to crush my good intention. Slowly cutting off the sunlight, in such precise measurements it's hard to tell if it's just getting dark outside sooner or if the sun really is dying. Instead you're a trophy on a shelf in your parents living room. And as much as I loved you, let's remember that Lucifer was once an angel too and you're killing me here.

when you left love became self-inflicted

Free falling from formality
Here's how he handled his hypocrisy
Beheading blackouts with brazen bravo
Testing trust with taciturn tendencies
Labyrinthine and lethargic logic
Whitewashed worries of wanton wars
Purchasing polluted policies of panacea
Equivocal empathy an emollient of the eagerness
Between the baleful borrowing of bedded bad's
Grasping, gasping, graphic
Aubades are an apostate anthem
My morning mouth messier than magnanimous
Salient and sardonic speech silenced by stalwart scars

you never asked for forgiveness because
you knew you didn't deserve it

I'd rather hurt myself. I'd rather understand the kind of pain I want – need – to fill me up than have you pretending. And this half-full concept leaves me half-empty to hope which burns me up and dries out what you give. The only thing you try is to tune me out because you don't like the truth that you are intune with me. With your half-insults, half-ignoring me, half-hitting home. I don't need any more halves in my life and you certainly aren't mine. Give me your all: all the anger, all the hate, all the self loathing, and truths that have become secrets. Or take all of your imcompletes and go home. I don't need you like the residue of smoke on my walls. Like the extra button I keep to a shirt I do not wear. You want the truth? I wish you made it as hard to hate you as you make it to love you.

For Two-Quarters You Can Have My Two Sense

What is so uninspiring
about an end
that I can never meet one
on good terms?

Is it knowing that
something else is
supposed to come but
never knowing if
it ever will?

Because even ends,
end. There is
a last for every finish,
and some...

we only get once.

And to be truthful,
I cannot name an
end that has been
more unkind to me
than I to it.

There are some ends,
I don't bother
to meet
at all.

Finish Line

you never communicated
write "I'm Sorry"
across my clit

———

You fuck her like your life source
is running on low
and leave her like you have somewhere to be.

You hold her like you want
to love her but
there's another lover you need to see.

*Dedicated to the men with little boys in their hearts that
made fools of them.*

Depression doesn't make a sudden appearance. It doesn't show up at your door unannounced after you kicked it out who knows how long ago. It's like a dog with its tail between its legs after eating away at your favourite memories, knowing it's done something wrong. You pat it on the head thinking it's learned it's lesson and wake up with it curled at the end of your bed. Soon it's eating your dreams instead and that's the thing about certain demons.. They find a way that will let you forgive them just to wrong you again. Each time it gets harder to push them away - each time sneaking in a little deeper before you realize what it's done. Making its way from your feet up to your pillow and asking you to stay in bed a little longer.

Some Things Are Not Lessons, Just Behaviours

You have never touched me but no-ones fingers haunt me more; memories of dreams, taunting me. But I'm glad you never did. My imagination is satisfying and I don't like being disappointed.

I Don't Like Being Disappointed

I AM ADDICTED TO STRANGERS. HOW THEIR LOVING
FEELS LIKE SOMETHING THAT WILL NEVER BE
FAMILIAR, HOW NICE IT IS TO HAVE TO FIT JUST
RIGHT IN THEIR ARMS ONLY ONCE. TO NOT HAVE TO
KNOW THEIR EYES OR THEIR MOTHERS NAMES. I AM
IN LOVE WITH THE QUIRKS THAT WILL NEVER HAVE
TO BURDEN ME IN THE FUTURE. I SEEK OUT THE
SOFT, FIRM LIPS THAT WILL NEVER DISAPPOINT ME
BECAUSE I EXPECT THEM TO LIE OR AT LEAST NOT
TELL THE TRUTH, AND ALL THEY WANT TO OFFER
ME IS EUPHORIA; LIPS THAT DO NOT TELL ME A
STORY BECAUSE THEY ARE CREATING ONE. I DO NOT
WANT TO KNOW THE WITHDRAWL OF KNOWING
ONE PAIR OF HANDS TOO WELL AGAIN. EACH TIME I
GET HIGH IT IS AS DIFFERENT AS THE DRUG I AM ON.
I DREAM OF TONGUES I DON'T KNOW AND THE
POWER OF KNOWING MYSELF SO DIFFERENTLY
FROM HOW THEY WANT TO KNOW ME.
WITHDRAWALS ARE UNNOTICED UNTIL I AM
LOOKING FOR A FIX IN MUSCLES. I HAVE NEVER
LEARNED TO IGNORE TEMPTATION, ONLY HOW TO
AVOID THE CONSEQUENCES. I APPEASE MY
CONSCIENCE WITH THEIR NAME BEFORE I LET GO.
HABITUALLY, I INDULGE IN NEW INFORMATION AND
THE FREE REIGN I HAVE OF MYSELF.

LIFE
THE WORLD AND ITS
FASCIA
4

Forest Fires

THE FIRST TIME I HEARD THIS TERM AND UNDERSTOOD IT I WAS ELEVEN, AND A RED HAIRED BOY WAS USING IT TO DESCRIBE WHAT I'M LIKE WHEN I GET MAD. IRONIC, HAS HE SEEN HIS HEAD?

YOU DON'T HAVE TO BE DRIED UP TO GET STRUCK BY LIGHTNING & CATCH FIRE.

BUT I HAVE BEEN DRY TOO. BEFORE. BUT LATER THAN ELEVEN IN MY LIFE SPAN TO KNOW THAT SOMETIMES PEOPLE LEAVE FIRES IN YOU UNATTENDED, AND YOU'VE BEEN WAITING FOR IT TO RAIN - SIMILAIR TO WAITING FOR THE SHOE TO DROP.

ANYWAY - HOWEVER EASY IT IS TO BECOME SUCH AN IGNITED VERSION OF MYSELF I NEVER BECOME BIG ENOUGH TO DO MUCH HARM. LIKE THAT FIRE I SAW IN A TREE, AFTER A STORM, IN HALIFAX. AND THE WOMAN THIS TREE BELONGED TO SAID, WHEN WE KNOCKED ON HER DOOR

"IT WAS WORSE BEFORE, THE FIRE DEPARTMENT WAS SUPPOSED TO GET HERE AN HOUR AGO?"

I DON'T REMEMBER THAT STORM AS SPECTACULAR BUT IT YIELDED WORSE RESULTS THAN ITS OWN TIME THERE.

REGARDLESS, THIS BUSINESS OF FOREST FIRES, DOES IT ACCOUNT FOR THINGS IGNITED BY LOVE? ARE SMUDGING AND SMOKING SIMILAR PRACTICES? BECAUSE I FEEL A LITTLE LESS EVERY DAY BUT MAYBE I AM GETTING CLEANED OUT.

BUT SOMETIMES MORE LIKE A CHIMNEY THAT NEEDS SWEEPING. I DON'T MEAN FUCKING. JUST AIR TO BREATH. BUT THERE ARE PRACTICES THAT PURPOSELY BURN THINGS DOWN SO NEW CAN GROW BETTER AND WHEN CAN YOU TELL THE DIFFERENCE BETWEEN INTENT AND UNATTENDED?

The sky is weeping. Trying to wash away all that has been committed on the ground. It's cold heart freezing the tears, as snow creates a blank canvas to build a better story. This is what we tell ourselves when the black paper sky is spoiled by stars, and we forget that the blackness was there first, as the blackness was here first. Yet we wash away a new year in a blanket of snow, believing that the colours of a suns routine will transfer over. But we come from the atmosphere, and the more we believe that white is the beginning, the more grey matter we have to alter. There is a reason midnight is a blank canvas, and not high-noon. There is a reason that snow melts, because what has happened can not be forgotten.

00:01 January 1st

You'd run the shower all night
if it sounded
like rain
on your window,

the clouds weeping happiness
that winters cold heart
had melted.

Loving us right through the bottom
of our feet and
the tops
of our heads,

letting us know that defrosting
is the first stage
in blooming.

Creaky stairs to the basement of my brain. The workshop desolate, covered in cobweb thoughts spun thin; unclean, unused, unbrushed. The terrors of the basement of my brain too hard to face. The memories stored in mis-happen boxes; unlabelled, unorganized, unopened. It will take days and years to purge myself of this space. It will days and years and broken dolls, black markers, old photographs, sun-bleached-fridge-posted-magnet-wrinkled-art, too small and too big clothing, notes from my grandfather and his wife - never received or never sent - it will take hours and months to make this space constructive. No one knows my possessions - the printed pages, stained and weathered by my fingers grasp and the salt of each time I held them and remembered and wept until I filed them from myself deep in the chambers of "nothing" where I keep secrets from myself. And in the attic are secrets of others. Not forgotten just buried under dust and boarded up windows that scream for light every time I peek my head through the doorway to see that there are no ghosts. No ghosts - that I clandestinely wish were there to seek their revenge or confess their sins, but all that's left are the imprints of my imagination like disfigured footprints on the grey ground. The imagination that brings alive the things kept under ground of what now strangers never told me and I am lost, lost, lost. But I open old trunks filled with skins of who I used to be and try them on for size. I play pretend with feelings of the past; in broken mirrors that caused me more than seven years of bad luck because there is nothing that can act as an emollient for my need for things to be how I wish they were so everything stayed sharp.

Nothing that can make what never happened better. And when I tire I lay down in blankets of old nightmares and pretend that they're your arms holding me instead because, really, it's the same thing at this point. It's all the same thing. The unwritten books under the creaky stairs and the worn out skins in broken dressers; paper thin in the thighs, too tight in the soul, loose in my control. Torn up sheets covering the outline of some places I may have been, and here I am...open, from when I screamed your name, and called his with the conviction that the jealousy it could create would bring you back. But I know you are lost as I am lost, in your own attic reading the words you could have wrote, flipping through pictures of memories never made, but at least you have that. The would haves and should haves. I'm left with the could haves and if-I-maybes and the tears and pain and I will never un-board these windows because I don't need to shed light on what I can't have. I already see enough of what I dread, and although the shadows scare me the dream that you're still hiding in them is enough for me to bear it.

it isn't often that a place shows it's used; places are not like people, we expect there to be dirt on the surface and can find beauty in the decrepit. but some places seem to have more meaning than what people gave it. this town, made to sustain those who stayed, and learned to never expect anything back. hot, flaking summers. golden and sucked dry by those who run the roads - those who never see it clean, and do not care if it finds a way to be replenished because they have their own wells to worry about.

with empty porches on corners, rocking chairs still waiting by windows that were never given the opportunity to be that hopeful because the cold makes them brittle or simply just drunks can be mean, and people want to see how much of the world they can take without owning it. but it was made to be this way. made to fall down a mountainside, slowly shrinking while tin buckets sit amongst the roots and mushrooms, long past their childhoods and no one thinks much of what is there - that it is common like the moss, not uncommon like our society. letting things be forgotten, falling down, not knowing they would one day need to support themselves. but we know how to support ourselves, tricks we never trade lest our opportunity lays in the hands of another.

still, they come just to leave better, packing light so they can bring back souvenirs. not caring that if everyone takes a brick, soon we have lost a home.

Dawson City

Summer legs that see more long grass and fence spokes than sun. More cool water stolen and sliding down shivering stomachs from dirty bleached out hair than warm sand sticking to the back of calves and shoulders. Skin coloured from bruises not UV rays. Never hydrated for all that is drank, every roof climbed helping you find your way to falling before flying. The most the sun is seen is in pink and purple splashes on the east horizon on a 5AM walk home. That is also the most that is remembered. Husky voices, poisoned insides, untainted mouths and bodies that feel more air and rain than they do clothes. Leaving you more dried out than the remnants of autumn leaves, finished faster than drunk words falling out of mouths.

The Season Dignity Was Undignified

When we see a tree bowed, hunched over in pain, do we think it any less strong in its misery? Has it's grief and age and experience diminished - not weathered - our shallow perceptions? No. We see it as valiant. As tried, stubborn, something without resolve in it's figure, but much compromise. Why do we not see ourselves in the same light? Holding our heads low from the injustice of it all, but holding our heads still nonetheless.

We Forget Our Roots

as slow as the dawn you stay
up all night for
more stickier than the dew
on petals that follows

as hard as the rain that falls
tonight and again
more gentler than the smell
on the streets

my favourite flowers hang
reminding me there are things
in life that don't remind me
of you

as fast as the cars out of control
on the wet pavement
more slower than the collisions

thunder commands my attention
seeks my affections, and
makes me one with the
wet weather

No More Reminders

You are aging. Even if you won't admit it, you're afraid. Like a young girl worried of losing her beauty to acne scars and kisses from the wrong boy - but back aches and wrong wives. The drugs you do won't amount to the adventures you used to have. It won't bring them back and not eating will just make you decay faster; the skin falling off your muscles while you realize there is no back bone to be found. There is nothing here for you and I know your motives. One last big move to bring everything back although the only thing the future holds for you is acceptance - but soon you'll forget that. You'll forget it all. Standing before me in too loose and too old fleece pyjamas, preaching to me about youth and art and beauty like I'm not the one representing it. Making desperate attempts in your speeches and rants to hide the terror that whittles away at you; life smoking you slowly like the joints you roll as we talk. But there is no high like the satisfaction that someone is looking through you because this old man before me knows better than anyone that we spend our whole lives perfecting our mask just to find someone who sees through it. I hope you were surprised when it was me. You used to be wild. Now you're just crazy. The man I thought you were has burned down to show me the man you are. I don't revere you. I don't look up to you. Although I listen, it's only because I've heard it before. Reckless and abandoned as you have ever been, you were the first to sense I would leave. There is nothing here for me like I imagined, just the same as you. But I can escape and I won't let you live vicariously.

So I sit with my patience and my drugs and listen - so much of you, and so little at the same time. We bike until there's no more breath (or for you, no more battery), and I already miss you. You don't know it. I already miss you because you know I won't have the time for it after this is over. But when you are quiet I don't miss you anymore, we're both gone & we both know it. In your too loose pyjama set, your too loose morals are set free when you tell me secrets I don't want to know. But they are mine now old man, mine to keep and breathe from because even though you are here, you are gone with the wind you try to shelter as you light another. There's no going back and no one to take you there. The wrong intentions with the right person. But also the right intentions with the wrong person. You had so much more coming for you and reality came in like a babysitter that life never fired - you just have to keep paying your dues. Constantly controlling your actions. These people that you love only because you have to, and me - the only one you loved because you couldn't help it. And I love you too, but it's because I want to. I hate you the same and it's something I can't prevent. I don't revere you. I am disappointed and I can't be bought, but Jesus know's you'll try - so does God if you believe in that - and I won't step in to stop you even though I'd be stepping back in line. Maybe that makes us the same. Or maybe it proves how different we are. It doesn't matter. You are lost and I am gone, but the difference is only one of us can come back. I don't think I will.

The Way it Feels To Be Mad at The Truth

She thinks about strangers and the way they make her feel poetry without words, falling in love until her eyes fall away - sometimes up to too many times a day. Feeling as easily as sun comes through a window; warm, stuffy, and claustrophobic. Ignorant to the breeze outside. She's a little more lost with a map, a little less tough with a frown. No rose petals falling from hips nor wisdom from a mouth, no gold from hair, or feathers from fingertips. She is just the kind to tell you with such conviction that her dreams are truths that you start to believe in the religion of her mind. Don't be fooled, salt water eyes will drown you not refresh you. She has a storm inside too strong to be seen on the horizon, no calm before because no-one ever taught her to be silent. Cursing life in the same tune she sings it, falling in love with strangers with gardens that need rain in their eyes.

Not What You See in The Mirror

When you sneeze I am suddenly aware that beside me you are having a 10th of an orgasm, and that the likelihood of you having the same thoughts about me as a stranger as I am having is high. There is intimacy in the fact that our legs are touching right now but scientifically nothing can touch. But even if that's true electricity still runs from lightning through a lake when it's thundering and I'm curious as to how many sneezes it would take to feel that way.

Transit Thoughts In Transition

My heart is one thousand years old,
and I can't let it go.
It aches in a way,
this young body doesn't know.

It does not stick to my sleeve,
I lost that ability.
I want to spread it's ashes
but it will not let me.

My heart is one thousand years old,
it won't let my spirit go.
It tells me it is scared
to go it alone.

Accelerated Aging

THE RAIN SAID DO NOT WORSHIP WATER
NO WHISPER OF WANTS CAN STOP
THE MAD MAN IN THE SKY AS HE SHOWS
THE MOON HE GARDENED SCREAMING LOVE
INTO SLEEPY DELIRIOUS LIES
TONGUING LIFE FROM GIRLS AS IF
THEY ARE MILK AND HONEY
LANGUID MEN LICKING SWEETLY
FROM THE SPRINGS HER DREAMS SWIM THROUGH
BLACK AND SMOOTH
WHERE NOW THEY TRUDGE DRUNK
AND LUSTLESS AND RAW
BENEATH THEM WE WERE ACHING
WITH DEATH AND REALITY
PREACHING TO THE MOON
AND REMEMBERING
DO NOT WORSHIP WATER
WE CAN DROWN, WE CAN FLOAT

Cultivating

Forest Greenwell is a young Canadian author. Poetry is her passion, but she also write for and runs the blog collective herHABITAT and has been featured on other select publications.
She currently resides and creates in Toronto, CA where she can be found painting, biking, talking to plants, and making coffee.

@forestgreenwell
forestgreenwell.ca

@herhabitatblog
herhabitat.ca

This book is an accumulation of more than 5 years of hurting, learning, love, and forgiving. It is comprised of every uplifting and suffocating experience I have had to date. Thank you for being a part of it. I hope something has stuck with you amongst these pages, or that at least a part of you was spoken to.

All my gratitude,

Forest Greenwell